DYING FOR I DO

Lessons Learned While Choosing
Self-Love Over Matrimony

DYING FOR I DO

Lessons Learned While Choosing
Self-Love Over Matrimony

Eunice Pierre-Louis

DEDICATION

"I knew I was going to love my daughter, but I had no idea how much I would love her."-Jeremy Sisto

To Mari- my wished-for child you are everything I didn't know I needed in my life. You are enough. I promise to believe you and trust your judgment.

ACKNOWLEDGMENTS

I want to start by thanking my younger siblings for believing in me and supporting me from the very beginning. Tilou, Fran and G, you are amazing and I love you.

Thank you to my sister cousin, Kizzy, for offering me your help, support and love.

To Jasmine Womack, my editor and publisher, you following your dreams helped me to follow mine.

To P31 Publishing for your patience and support in bringing my vision to life.

CONTENTS

A Frightening Realization

SLAM!

The sound of his fist hitting the wall less than five inches from my face coupled with the absolute rage in his eyes was exactly what I needed to snap out of my waking nightmare. I finally had to admit what I had been trying to hide from. I felt a coldness in the pit of my stomach. There could be no wedding. I knew with abject certainty and dread that if I married this man in three weeks it would not be a fairytale ending. Saying I do would be the death of me.

He was going to kill me. I was as certain of this as I was my own name.

How did I get here?

CHAPTER 1

THE BEGINNING

I was born in Haiti and spent the first half of my life living in Miami. As a first-generation child of an immigrant, life was certainly different than what I saw on tv and read in my books. My mother worked what felt like a million hours a week and we were told CONSTANTLY that education was all we had to worry about here in AMERICA. No boys, no parties, no fashion. Study and become a doctor, lawyer or nurse.

Let me tell you, by twenty-seven, I was a major disappointment to my parents. Actually I had the entire family dismayed. I had no degree, no husband and no children. I was living the plot of the film, My Big Fat Greek Wedding.

It was a constant point of contention. I was an old maid in my family. It didn't help that I had cousins getting married every other year. It also didn't help that I was always a bridesmaid and never a bride.

I'd gotten to the point where I didn't even want to date if it wasn't going toward marriage. I'd always said that I didn't want the wedding as much as I wanted everything that came after. I couldn't wait for my happy ending but only if it was true love. I really believed that I would find a man that was perfect for me, that would love me for me and that I would flourish with. Every time one of my friends or cousins got engaged, I added a new item to my list of things that would prove I'd made the right choice. I was convinced that I could not make a wrong choice in a spouse. I was too smart. I was too practical.

I was wrong.

When Man* showed up with all of his promises of a bright future, I believed him. After all I 'knew him', right? In the beginning everything was beautiful. We spoke on the phone for hours. He would text me good morning every single day. He sent daily jokes. We watched the same movies on Netflix together even though we were hundreds of miles apart.

CHAPTER 2

THE REUNION

Everyone always wants to know how we met. How did I not know the kind of person he was? How could I be fooled so? Well, let me tell you how.

This story begins when we were in middle school. Man was the older brother of one of my closest friends. I knew him mostly in passing. He was a couple of grades ahead of me I believe. The way I was raised, even if I'd noticed him as anything than my friends' brother nothing would have happened. We reunited years later through social media. He would often reach out to see how I was doing and to let me know of fake pages that were using my pictures. I'd begun modeling a bit by then and it was just an expected thing you could say. We never spoke much outside of that, but we kept in contact.

Of course, life goes on and we lived our separate lives.

During this time I had relocated back to South Florida from Atlanta. I lived with my younger sister near a few cousins and aunts. I had a great support system in place.

Shortly after my 28th birthday Man began reaching out to me more often. I found the timing to be interesting because I'd been praying for someone who was serious to come my way.

I said God, "I'm not looking, send me my husband when you're ready."

There were a couple of interested guys, but Man was persistent, and I'd 'known' him nearly half my life. Pretty soon there were late-night phone conversations, video calls, constant daily texts. We were living in different states but we were constantly in contact. I was quickly smitten.

For our first '*date*' Man flew to my city. He even met all of my family in South Florida. He was a complete gentleman and charmed everyone, young and old alike. We ended the night at the beach, talking until the sun came up. It was beautiful. Honestly, it was like a well-scripted scene in a romantic movie.

When he started speaking of marriage after less than a year, I thought it was fast but not unreasonable. After all, I was *SO* old and I couldn't really afford to wait. Right?

Early on Man started to speak of me moving to the Midwest where he was. He wanted us to be closer and to grow as we worked toward marriage. I informed him that I was not a fan of shacking up but I would be willing to get married at the courthouse before we had a large traditional ceremony if we went to couples counseling first. I thought for sure this was the smart way to do it. I had covered all my bases, or so I thought. When

Man offered to fly me to his city so that I could prepare to move I was fully on board. I began searching for a job and soon was interviewing for a great position near where he worked. I flew out to do my final interviews and look at apartments. I was so excited. Man offered to pay for my flight when I moved officially. We began to make plans for our future. I was ecstatic. Everything was perfect. It didn't take long to realize that things weren't as great as I thought.

Lesson learned: If it seems too good to be true it is ok to be skeptical.

CHAPTER 3

THE FIRST RED FLAGS

We fought my very first night in the city. He was upset that we were staying at the hotel that I would be working at. He felt that it wasn't very private because my new coworkers would be in our business. He thought that we should have gotten a hotel room somewhere else while we waited for our new apartment to get ready. I didn't understand the reasoning then and I still don't understand it now. I just remember being near tears as I tried to ask him if he really thought it was best that we spend more money when we were waiting for an apartment to be ready and pay deposits, move-in fees and what have you. As I struggled to fall asleep that night, I tried to rationalize it as just nervous jitters as we prepared to merge our lives together.

Three days later when I mentioned the money for my ticket since I was needing to buy things to get situated in my new city, he blew up! He said he'd never even asked me to move. That he didn't invite to come here. He maintained that he never offered to pay for my ticket. I WAS FLOORED. I called my baby sister the next morning at work. She was just as shocked. She reminded me that he'd said the same to her. She asked me if I was coming back home? I really thought about it. I really did. I had just gotten a new job and I was sure it was a misunderstanding. I couldn't just quit.

Maybe I could just stay on-site at the hotel? Maybe I shouldn't have said anything? This was my first experience with gaslighting. For anyone who is unfamiliar with how abusers work, gaslighting is a tactic in which a person, in order to gain more power, makes a victim question their reality. After work that day he was so apologetic. He gave me a story about being embarrassed and wanting to make it up to me. I let him. After all, who holds a grudge after receiving a sincere apology? At least I thought it was sincere.

When I started to talk about how this relationship grew, I found that I made a lot of excuses. I had a lot of explanations. In hindsight, it was pretty bad very early on. I like to say that we only fought every few months as most normal couples would. That was true. I was too busy trying to not upset him. The blowups would come when I let my guard down or when some new things unexpectedly set him off.

So, this book isn't about a bad break up. We've all been there. I'm sharing this in hopes that if you have found yourself in a similar situation you don't waste your time rationalizing and making excuses like I did. Run. It only gets worse.

One of the things he began doing almost from the start was to try to restrict who I was in contact with. He always seemed to have an explanation for why it was a bad time for my sister, cousins or friends to call. Mind you he could be on the phone as early or as late or as often as he wanted with anyone. He swore that all of my male friends secretly liked me or that I had had previous relationships with them that I was hiding from him. It was a little flattering at first that he thought that I was so attractive EVERYONE wanted me. It didn't take long for me to realize that wasn't what he meant.

When we were choosing the wedding photographer he was vehemently against my choice. I was floored. My choice was an amazingly talented, highly sought-after world-renowned artist. Everyone we asked sided with me when they saw his work. Still, he refused. Finally, after I'd had enough, I demanded an answer as to why he was so against my choice.

He said it was because I modeled professionally. I was so confused by this reasoning. If anything, that would mean I could make a better choice, I thought. He elaborated that everyone knows that models and photographers sleep together.

"Do you mean have relationships? Because I've never dated the photographer," I explained to no avail. He then explained that it was his belief that all models slept with all their photographers. I asked him if he'd slept with his photographers when he ventured into modeling.

"It's different for men," he said with a straight face, while looking directly into my eyes. I didn't even think before I asked him why he even wanted to marry me if he felt that way and believed that women were like cars and were more valuable with fewer miles.

Another chance to run that I missed. He later back peddled and I believed him when he said that's not what he meant. He frequently lied about saying things and later changed his mind as if he'd never said the original statement.

Another red flag that I missed was when he started acting out on his expectations of a wife. (Side note: don't do wife things for non-husbands.) He wanted me to take care of our home which we had previously discussed but he also expected me to work full time which at the time was 50 hours a week. Then he wanted to split all of the bills in half.

I'm sure that arrangement works for some people, but that's not what we had discussed when we were speaking of expectations and the role of a husband or a wife. We'd spoken at length about his old fashioned expectations. I was to keep the house and he was to be the primary financial provider. According to him, he'd never said that, even though he told all of my friends and family and siblings that he wanted to come in and take care of me. I don't think anyone's definition of take care of includes a 50 hour work week plus cooking every meal. More gaslighting here. He said that wasn't the deal. His money wasn't where it used to be. He needed a helpmate who wouldn't leave when times get hard. I found myself thinking that for better or worse meant that marriage would not be all roses and champagne so we could work through this. Meanwhile, I began to resent doing all the cooking, cleaning, shopping, and budgeting as well as paying any non-budgeted popup bills even if the expense was not my own.

I later learned that even though he expected all of this from me he continued to insinuate to others that he was the kind of man who would take care of his partner.

It was important to him that he be seen and perceived in a particular way. I found myself wanting to help him project that image. So I didn't complain. I didn't tell anyone what was happening. I wouldn't admit that everything wasn't great. I thought that we could fix things. I worried that if I complained or admitted how terrible it was that I wouldn't be able to move forward if things did improve. I did not want anyone to be able to say that I had not made a good choice. Unfortunately, that's what it was. I had made a poor choice. If I'm being honest, I was also embarrassed. I thought admitting my mistake in choice of a partner would make me look foolish and quite frankly, stupid.

Lesson learned: Speak up. Don't shrink yourself for anyone. When you start to see the inconsistencies, don't pretend they aren't there. It helps no one.

CHAPTER 4

THE EXCUSES

Hindsight really is 20/20. It is so easy to see where I went wrong. So easy to understand my mistakes when looking back. I will try to explain these mistakes to you as best I can without sugar-coating things with the insight I now have.

Unfortunately, I was not the only person making excuses for him. Once his family had a get together with his parents, brother, sister-in-law and sisters. His father was in town and had initiated the meeting. The meeting was to work out why he was angry with his sister-in-law. Seeing this interaction first hand, I realized that his family was also making excuses for him.

During the conversation he became upset with his sister-in-law and chased her out of a room. I told myself he was just angry. When his brother and two of his sisters had to restrain him, I couldn't believe my eyes.

He chased a woman out of the room. A woman who was related to him by marriage to his own brother. He was yelling threats of bodily harm. He didn't care that his whole family was there. Hearing his niece and nephew scream and cry while he tried to get at that their mother did not deter him. His own brother having to hold him back meant nothing to him. This shook me out of my excuses. He was a dangerous man. If I wasn't careful, this would be my future. It was as if he would be willing to fight his family to get to the woman he was upset with. Clearly no one wanted to see this happen. It wasn't as if they all just sat around and let him get to her. When they were able to calm him down his brother left with his family. Nothing was resolved that night.

I remember going to sit in his sisters' room and looking up cab companies on my phone. I felt like I was on autopilot. I was doing the things that my mind was saying I should do. In actuality, I felt numb, like I was just going through the motions. He followed me into the room and asked what I was doing. When I told him he became dismissive. He felt like if I called the cab company I should just call off the wedding. At this point I was ready to do just that and said so before he left the room.

His mother entered the room shortly after he left. She sat with me and spoke at length. She told me about her own relationship with his father. She told me about his anger issues and things about his childhood. She spoke about how kind and caring he was underneath it all. Listening to his dear sweet mother making excuses for his behavior actually weakened my resolve. After all, who knows him better than his family?

This is the danger in looking for the best in people. I wanted so badly to believe that he was a good person. If I admitted that he wasn't so great I would have to admit that I had made a poor choice. I know I've mentioned this before but I'm not sure if it was clear. I honestly believe that admitting that I'd made a poor choice would be akin to admitting failure, or defeat.

I understand now that I am not defined by my relationship status. I wish that was something I understood at the time. Realy, I wish that was the end of this book. That I could tell you how I walked away at this point.

Spoiler alert. I did not leave after this.

Lesson learned: Don't let anyone talk you into staying in bad relationships, not even yourself.

CHAPTER 5

THE HONEYMOON PHASE

The weeks following this ultra-violent, eye-opening incident were like a dream. He went out of his way to be very sweet and almost apologetic for his behavior. I say almost apologetic because a true apology includes admitting you are wrong followed by changed behavior. He would never admit any wrong doing but his behavior would momentarily improve. I honestly could not stay upset. It felt like he was trying to sweep me off my feet all over again. It was mostly just sweet words and spending time not arguing. There were smiles and laughs. We didn't speak of that incident and I chose to continue moving forward with my wedding plans.

I will take this time to point out that this phase is quite common in all sorts of abusive relationships. This is the stage where the abuser places blame on others and makes apologies or promises to change.

In the year of planning and preparation leading up to our wedding we had quite a few blow-ups followed equally as often by honeymoon or reconciliation phases. As we got closer to the wedding, the blow-ups came far more often and the sweet lulls between got shorter and shorter.

During some of these sweet phases, I found myself lowering my guard. I believed that his angry, hateful behavior was the anomaly. This wonderful, sweet person who was going out of his way to make me laugh and feel comfortable could not possibly be terrible. I could hardly believe that this man was the same as the one who could spend days alternating between ignoring me and berating me for simple perceived mistakes.

These happy times were enough to make me start making excuses every time some new treacherous or horrible behavior was exhibited. I used these happier times to convince myself that I had in fact made a good decision in my choice of a future spouse.

When he was kind, I told myself that this was the real him. This was the guy I'd said yes to. When he did sweet things like get me flowers or pay me compliments, I would use this to justify my staying.

After leaving this relationship I read and researched domestic violence in relationships. I was able to understand that I was not alone in using the happy moments to justify staying. So if you are going through this or have gone through this, please know that you are not alone.

Lesson learned: It's ok to hold people accountable for their behavior, even yourself. When the bad outweighs the good it isn't healthy.

CHAPTER 6

MORE RED FLAGS

I don't want to turn this into a woe is me tale. I will be listing examples of things that happened that were not ok but I will not be listing every slight and aggression.

The bad behavior got to be so common that I honestly just began trying to avoid conflict or upsetting him at all costs. I told myself that keeping a happy home was about compromise. I tried to get myself to believe that if I could predict the things that would cause a fight that I would be able to avoid the fights. That was never the case.

I was allegedly guilty of a myriad of infractions and I could never keep up.

If I overslept and didn't make breakfast before waking him, I could look forward to the silent treatment that day. If left work a few minutes late it was a capital offense. If I served leftovers for lunch there would be a row!

I was heading to work one Sunday, a day I didn't normally work. He flew into a rage and accused me of trying to meet someone for a romantic tryst. By now I was accustomed to his antics so I asked him if he would like to come with me. I told him that it wouldn't take long. He was adamant that he didn't want to waste his time at my job. I explained to him that this was my job. Any time I was able to work extra or to exceed my performance expectations would be good for us both. For some reason that I still don't know, he then switched gears. He started by saying that he was angry because he was worried about me. He continued by saying that my pants were too tight and he didn't want me to leave the house in them. He was worried that I would be raped because I had on these pants. It didn't matter that I was dressed appropriately to go to work. It did not seem to make a difference to him. I was at a loss as to how he thought that my going to work an extra day was *certain* to result in my being raped. After a rather lengthy and frustrating exchange where he informed that sometimes rape isn't really rape. I just gave up on getting any work done that day.

Many of our arguments ended in this way with me just giving in to keep the peace. It was better, I felt, to just acquiesce rather than continue to fight.

Another time, less than three months before the wedding, I accidentally swiped our shared credit for a purchase instead of my debit card. The total was thirteen dollars and some change. Nothing that would break the bank. I thought nothing of it. I was not ready for the fight that would follow.

He came to my job. He stood at the front desk and began bellowing at me. I was caught completely off guard. He tore into me about trying to ruin his credit. He claimed that the balance rolling over into the next statement period would cause his credit score to drop. I tried to explain that that wasn't how credit worked.

Nothing I said could calm him down. I kept worrying that one of my guests or employees would hear him. I was fighting tears at this point. Nothing could calm him down. He kept getting louder and angrier. I was happy to be behind the desk as I tried in vain to hold back the tears. After a few minutes of this my assistant manager came in from her smoke break and stood behind me. She looked at him and crossed her arms. He looked from her to me and back to her. He told me he'd see me later.

As soon as he left she gave me a hug. "You don't have to go home with him." Her words opened the floodgates and the tears came pouring out. I spent the next couple of hours alternating between crying and raging to his mother and mine. We were a little over two months out from our wedding. I was livid and hurt! I kept trying to make them understand how disrespected and disgusted I felt. I hid in one of the rooms and cleaned. I was too embarrassed to show my face at the front desk.

Both of our mothers tried to convince me that it wasn't that bad. As if a thirteen dollar transaction was worth this kind of strife. I reasoned that if he was acting like this for a dollar store purchase what would he do when we had a mortgage? What if we had children? What of the expenses that come with rearing a child?

This was not ok. The pit that was growing in my stomach could not be stilled.

I. Was. Done.

That evening I did go home with him despite all protests and warnings from my assistant manager. In a last-ditch effort to change my mind, she told me that she was worried he might kill me and that I should walk away now. Her warning sent a chill down my spine, but I didn't listen, not that day.

The ride home was silent. We shared a car because he always said it was more cost effective. I'd long since realized that it was more so to control and restrict my ability to move independently. I'm sure he thought this was going to go the way of most of our arguments but I wasn't going to cower today.

Once in the house he began to argue again. I raged right back. After nearly an hour he let it be known that he didn't think we should get married. I agreed wholeheartedly. He decided that he was spending the night in the guest bedroom. I didn't mind one bit. I spent the night going over my options. Sure it would be embarrassing to start over, but it wouldn't be the end of the world I reasoned.

The following day I returned the silent treatment that I regularly received. By lunchtime, he was ready to speak. I told myself nothing he said could change my mind. He swore he'd do anything to make up for the previous day's outburst and move forward. I agreed to speak to a counselor or pastor. If he could convince them that we should be married I would move forward. I couldn't see him getting anyone to agree. At this point I knew I wouldn't be happy in a marriage with him but I didn't feel I had any options outside of making the best of it.

We did see a counselor. We had one tear-filled session after which he promised that everything would be better. I wasn't sure how that would work but I heard him out. I told myself I could try if he did. Spoiler alert, nothing changed.

Lesson learned: sometimes outsiders see the truth, even when you don't want to acknowledge it. It's ok to listen to that feedback.

CHAPTER 8

THE TRUTH

Our daily routine became a string of nonarguments. He'd say or do something. I'd agree with it. He'd ask if I meant it. I'd always say yes. Keeping the peace in such a manner is exhausting and isn't actually sustainable.

I know that he knew I wasn't being sincere but short of picking more fights there wasn't much he could do. Every day I would wake up and remind myself that I just had a short time left before the wedding. Then I'd remember that after "I do" comes forever.

Every place I turned and every person I knew would ask how the wedding planning was going and then casually bring up cold feet. I was beginning to think that my trepidation was just that, cold feet. An absolutely normal, even reasonable, reaction.

The truth was something else entirely. The truth was that I was petrified. I knew that this was wrong but everywhere I turned I was being told to suck it up. I was told that I was being sensitive. I was even admonished for being ungrateful, after all, I was to be married soon.

That became crystal clear to me the day we had our last blow up before the wedding. I couldn't begin to tell you what started the argument. I know that all the agreeing and sniveling I was doing wasn't making a difference. He kept needling me. I couldn't hold back any longer and I lashed out in retaliation.

The level of his response was so unexpected. I'm not sure why I didn't see it coming but I didn't. I got up to go to the bedroom. He followed me. I turned around to inform him that today wasn't the day to do this. That's when he got in my face so I had nowhere to go but against the wall. We were so close that anyone walking in would probably think we were about to share a passionate kiss. Needless to say, that was not the case.

SLAM!

The sound of his fist hitting the wall less than five inches from my face coupled with the absolute rage in his eyes was exactly what I needed to snap out of my waking nightmare. I finally had to admit what I had been trying to hide from. I felt a coldness in the pit of my stomach. There could be no wedding. I knew with abject certainty and dread that if I married this man in three weeks it would not be a fairytale ending. I had no more excuses. I knew in every fiber of my being that saying I do to this man would be the death of me. That was the God's honest truth. I felt such a clear understanding at that moment. I couldn't change. I could not force this. It simply was not meant to be. At this point, I chose to walk away. I was going to go lay down. I had some things to figure out. He followed me down the hall antagonizing me. I was so over it all. I was so frustrated. "What are you going to do? What?" I yelled. I was putting on a brave face but I thought for sure that was a dumb move. I did it anyway.

I could not have guessed what was going to happen next in my wildest dreams. He pulled out his phone and made a call. He placed it on speaker. Who was he calling? When I heard the person on the other end I was floored. Could my living nightmare get any worse?

"911 what's your emergency?"

"Y'all can come get her. She won't shut up." That's exactly what he said.

"Excuse me, sir. What's your emergency?"

"She won't shut up." He repeated it.

"Please hang up." I was practically begging. I couldn't believe he would risk my freedom and safety over not getting his way. I knew I wouldn't be arrested for talking as it were. Yet as a black woman, I was afraid of the police escalating a minor situation with deadly force. Really, I realized he was risking himself as well. After all, black men die at the hands of police far too often for comfort. Who knows how the police would react if they came?

I made my way onto my bed and sent his sister a text asking her to come get me. PLEASE. She called me immediately. I couldn't hold back the tears. She said she was on her way. Less than two minutes later he walked into the room and informed me that if she came here he had no problem beating her ass too.

I was shaken. Too? Was that his way of telling me he planned on being physical? Was that his plan? What had I gotten myself into?!

I called her back and basically begged her not to come. I said we were working it out. I lied through my tears and fear. I called my mother. She wasn't helpful. She told me that if I didn't go through with the wedding she would let all of our family know that they shouldn't come. She guilted me about all of the people who were flying in from around the world to celebrate this day with me. I couldn't take it. I called one of my married cousins. This isn't normal I told her. I cried through our entire conversation. She told me it could work but not if I was afraid there was nothing to work out. She was quiet for a minute and asked if needed a way out. She offered me her credit card.

I will always be eternally grateful to her for that answer.

I was working on the beginnings of a plan. I told her I would be fine but I appreciated her.

My next call was to my baby sister. I told her that I wasn't sure how but I knew I couldn't marry him. I would be home soon I told her. He came in and began railing at me about who was on the phone. He then began to pull all of my clothing off of the hangers in the closet and threw them onto the floor. I felt so small and trapped as I cried and tried to straighten up my clothes. This wasn't it. I would not live like this.

Lesson learned: You can't force a relationship no matter how hard you try. Choose relationships and spaces where you can blossom.

CHAPTER 9

THE PLAN

The next day I went to work and started on my plan. I called one of my old managers and asked if the company was hiring. I let her know that I'd be back in Atlanta in just a few weeks. I'd be ready to interview and could start as soon as I touched down. She said, of course, they'd find a position for me. That was one obstacle down.

That day I put in my two-week resignation notice. To my surprise, my new area massager accepted it, effectively immediately. I was upset at first but then I was thankful. That allowed me to put part two of my plan in motion. I went to the hardware store to get supplies. I needed boxes, packing tape and bubble wrap. I needed pack up my life. Then I went home and packed the majority of my things. I took all of the boxes to the post office and shipped them to my mother's. I called my sister to give her a heads up that my things were coming.

When I picked him up for lunch as was our usual custom, I let him know that I was no longer employed. I didn't have the option of not picking him up since we were still sharing the car. It even occurred to me to lie about my job. I had to be honest though since he was always my ride home. Our routine was that I would drive us to work and pick him up when we went to lunch. He would then take the car to work and pick me up at the end of my workday since he was off first. Of course, the news about my job was yet another argument. I knew I was leaving so I just agreed with all he said and apologized. He seemed shocked but he went with it.

When he returned to work, I called the wedding planner to inform her that I wouldn't be going through it. I wanted to know my options. She let me know that a marriage is only valid if the marriage certificate is filed in a timely fashion. That's how I decided on the final part of my plan. I knew that I had no intention of actually marrying him even if we did the ceremony. I called my sister and told her what to expect. My things would arrive before me. I would follow within a week. We would do the whole thing as planned but her job was to destroy and discard the marriage certificate after we'd signed it. There would be a wedding for all intents and purposes it would just be a party.

The actual ceremony was pretty much paid for. I saw no point in upsetting everyone by not having the ceremony. After all, if we got married and later divorced those same people would have still been at the wedding with us. I mean people wish you the best but they know not all marriages will make it. That's what I told myself anyway.

So that was it. That was my not so brilliant plan. I knew that we would fight after the ceremony so that was my secret way out. Yes, we would have a wedding. No, we would not be married.

I spent the next two weeks doing a lot of nodding and smiling. I just wanted to make it back to Atlanta safely.

Lesson learned: It's never too late to have an exit strategy. You can change your mind at any time.

CHAPTER 10

THE WEDDING

I flew into Atlanta first. So I began to put all the pieces of my plan into motion. Four days before the wedding we got into a huge argument, as expected. I used a word he didn't like. He accused me of trying to 'use big words' to make him feel small and stupid. He then informed me that he would be staying in the midwest and would not be coming for the wedding.

I was LIVID. I didn't put up with all of his crap just for him to change his mind now! Ridiculous, I know, but that was how I felt. Did I want to be tied to him for the foreseeable future? Absolutely not. We were less than a week away from the end of it. We just had to get through the event. Without paperwork it wouldn't be official so it wasn't going to be a real wedding but it would look like it. I knew he was going to initiate a fight soon after the vows but I didn't expect him to do it before. My mother, his mother, my cousins, it felt like everyone was taking turns trying to convince him to come.

The annoyance I felt transformed into rage. Why should anyone have to be cajoled into marrying me? More proof that we were not meant to be. Who needs to be convinced to marry someone they love? I knew that I didn't want to be his wife but I also knew that I expected this to look like the real thing. The whole point of this was to pretend everything was alright until it was safe to admit it wasn't.

He did finally show up on the day before our Saturday wedding. He almost missed our rehearsal because his best man was hungry and wanted to go eat on the other side of town. So they did that instead of coming to the rehearsal first. They got there forty minutes late. I wanted to be upset but it was to be expected at this point. That's right, you read that correctly. It was more important to him that the best man try a new restaurant than to be on time to our wedding rehearsal. As a result of his tardiness to said rehearsal we were unable to get to the courthouse to get our marriage license.

I considered that a blessing.

My wedding dawned bright and cheery. All I could think of was how it was almost over. Soon I'd be able to go back to my life. My old single life. I never thought I'd miss that life but I did. I finally understood that a partner wasn't the only thing it took to be happy. A partner could add to your sense of happiness but simply having someone wasn't the answer. I realize that I was being extremely naive. I really thought that it would be a clean break. I do one day, I don't the next.

While my makeup artist completed the final touches on my face, the officiating pastor came in to ask where the marriage certificate was. When I told him that we didn't have one he seemed shocked. He let me know that without that piece of paper we were just having a nice party. I told him I understood completely. He even mentioned that he might not perform the ceremony. I held my breath. Hoping he wouldn't. Alas, that wasn't meant to be. The pastor did decide to officiate our charade.

My wedding was beautiful and expensive and it wasn't at all what I wanted.

Even our first dance was a mockery of my 'dream' wedding. He insisted that he go out and dance alone first before I joined him. He wanted a moment in the spotlight before our guests saw and acknowledged us as a couple. I wish I were joking about that.

Overall the wedding itself was quite an affair. Our friends and family enjoyed themselves and everything was beautiful. It was almost nice enough for me to get sucked back into the fantasy of our relationship.

Almost. In the past when I've shared this part I've been asked if we cancelled our honeymoon. There was no need to. We had no honeymoon planned because he had wanted to do a boys trip the month before the wedding. That trip didn't happen and neither did our honeymoon. He left the following afternoon to take care of some previous responsibilities that simply could not be postponed or rescheduled to accommodate what was supposed to be the beginning of our official lives together. And thus the countdown to the end began.

Lesson learned: You deserve someone who puts you first in their decision making. It isn't too much to expect to be a priority in your partner's life.

CHAPTER 11

THE SEPARATION

It took less than three days for the fight that I knew was coming. He called me and he didn't like how I responded to a question he asked. He blew up!

The tirade went something like this:

"I knew I shouldn't have married you! This is the worst mistake of my life. I want a divorce. No! I want an annulment!"

He went on like this for a few minutes. When he finally took a breath I told him that would not be necessary.

"What do you mean?" he asked.

"We aren't married," I replied.

I tried my best to explain to him that no matter how many vows were spoken or where we said them, we were not married. Of course, he didn't believe me. I tried to explain about the marriage certificate. Still, he did not believe.

I finally ended the conversation by letting him know that his wish was granted, and he would not have to worry about me as a wife. I hung up and cried tears of joy. It was over.

Obviously, it wasn't that easy. I don't know what delusion I was under. He began to call repeatedly. I blocked him. He reached out to my family. Starting first with my mother. He laid it on thick. She became his biggest cheerleader and supporter. Then my older sister. Later my aunt and cousins. The many calls he made and messages sent made no mention of his wanting an annulment or wishing he'd never met me.

After a while most of my family and friends stopped accepting his calls and messages. Especially those who were his social media friends. They began to realize that the lovesick tale he was weaving did not match the slanderous online campaign he was waging against me. Luckily I wasn't privy to the majority of it but I was sent a few screenshots. It wasn't pretty.

During this time it felt like I was being pressured from all sides. I hated it. I made it a point to stay connected with the people who believed and supported me. This connection helped me to stand fast by my decision. I did eventually start taking his calls again in hopes that he would leave my family and friends out of it. No such luck. During this time he even told someone close to me that he often had to restrain himself to keep from slapping me.

When his words were revealed to me, I was floored. Why would he feel comfortable enough to say that? How was that 'proof' of his love? It was clear he was pushing for reconciliation for no reason other than wanting to be the one who controlled the trajectory of our relationship.

During this time he did several foul, unbelievable and disrespectful things. According to him it was all justifiable though. Usually, his favorite excuse to fall back on was that he was angry. Nothing new there.

During a conversation with him where I was trying to understand why he was even fighting the breakup, he called me a bitch. It took a moment for me to process what he said. I even asked him if he meant to call me a bitch. I was certain he would backpedal or make an excuse. Instead, he stood firm in the use of that language because, "I called you a bitch 'cause you're being a bitch."

I took this as further confirmation that I'd made the right choice. I didn't speak to him or accept any communications from him for a few days after that. When I did finally take his call, I inquired if he was calling to apologize. He wanted to know what for. When I informed him that I was still waiting for the apology for him calling me out of my name, he stuck to his original stance. He said it because he meant it so there would be no apology. I let him know I understood completely and disconnected the call.

There was no reasoning with the unreasonable. Over the next couple weeks he sent flowers via my aunt and edible arrangements via my mother. I felt like I was fighting on all sides. I was beginning to drown in a heavy blue funk. Would I never be rid of him? Whatever he was saying to them never included the threats he made when I was at work. The promises to just show up and 'fix' things. I was at my wit's end. I found myself taking his calls just so I wouldn't have to hear whatever he was saying second hand. Ignoring him increased the input from the people who he had convinced that he was so in love. Taking his calls further aggravated me and made me feel like I was losing my mind. Logic didn't work, being irrational didn't work, I was at my wits end. This was supposed to be the easy part. I had run out of ways to say that it was over.

One day when I was nearing an emotional breaking point I had a question for him.

"Since you want to be together now, answer one question for me. What do you like about me?"

I wouldn't accept his answers about physical attributes so I asked him again to name one single thing that he liked about me, as a person. You would have thought that I asked him to explain Einstein's theory of relativity in Mandarin. The next few times he called, I just asked him that and that would be the end of the conversation.

It was great to finally start to see the light at the end of this tunnel after the last couple of months of turmoil.

Lesson learned: Your experience is your own and it is valid. Your loved ones may think they are doing what's right for you. You know better than anyone what is right for you. Trust your instinct.

CHAPTER 12

THE FINAL ROW

I was naive to think that it would end so easily or so peacefully. There would be no civilized ending to this.

It had been a fairly uneventful October day. I had just hopped into bed in preparation for the early day I had ahead of me. Shortly before I dozed off there was a knock at my bedroom door. It was my brother. I don't remember what arbitrary thing he wanted to talk about but it didn't take long. Immediately after he left another knock came. Wondering what he may have forgotten, I shouted for him to come in. The light switched on and my heart jumped to my throat and dropped into my stomach. I couldn't believe my eyes. What was Man doing here? We stared at each other for a few seconds that felt like, to me anyway, an eternity.

"What? No smile? Aren't you happy to see me?"

That was all it took to snap me out of my reverie. I didn't believe I was actually seeing him in the same state as I was, much less in my bedroom. Hearing his voice made it real.

I asked him to leave the room so that I could get dressed. That request upset him. After all, he reasoned he'd seen me in varying states of undress before. I didn't care. Those days were gone and I needed him out while I gathered myself and dressed.

What in the world? I was staying in my mother's guest room which was on the first floor by the front door. When I stepped out my mother was sitting on the steps. One look at her face and I knew that she had something to do with this. She didn't seem shocked at all. I later found out that she had in fact been a part of this travesty. She'd worked out the details with him and somehow convinced herself that it was a great idea. My mother isn't a bad person. He's just that good at manipulating people. In her mind he couldn't be that bad because he had not actually put his hands on me. I saw it as something that was inevitable. She seemed to feel that that was not the case. She had good intentions but we all know the road to hell is paved with good intentions. Both of my sisters were at the top of the stairs. He immediately walked up close to me. I moved back until my back hit the closed door.

I asked him to back up. He took another step forward. I began to feel myself tensing up. I repeated myself. Louder this time.

"Back up off me!" I shouted. This brought my brothers into the hallway from the living room. I could tell that they were waiting for the slightest provocation so that they could step forward. I didn't want to start an altercation but I didn't want him this close either. He leaned forward and asked if my brothers were going to beat him up. I looked around at my whole family watching me and him still being in my face. I really wasn't sure what I should do. I didn't want to back down but I didn't need this escalating.

As the tension grew my oldest sister came flying down the stairs. She was seven months pregnant. She jumped between us and yelled for me to get back into the room. She followed me in and asked that I not speak with him. She reasoned that he seemed angry enough to get physical even with my family there. She now believed that I had made the correct choice in walking away. I tried to calm myself. I had to do something. I stepped back out of the room. I asked him to please step outside and I would meet him there to talk.

That request was not taken well. I asked again and my brothers each stepped closer. He decided to go outside. I used this time to call his brother. He knew his brother better than anyone. I was hoping that he could explain his motivation to me. Or maybe he could give me some kind of code word to diffuse the situation. He informed me that he had lent his brother the money to fly into Atlanta so he could make a last-ditch romantic effort to win me over. I didn't want to have a conversation with him but I knew I had to.

I stepped into the cool night air and steeled myself for the disaster to come. He immediately began by asking me if my brothers were gonna beat him up. I asked him what it was he wanted to talk about. I knew that I wasn't exactly alone since my family was just on the other side of the door. I also knew from experience that that wouldn't make much of a difference if he did try to get physical.

The conversation started innocently enough. He tried to get me to say that I missed him. That I wanted him back. When I wouldn't he said he missed me and wanted his wife back. I couldn't stop myself from reminding him that I wasn't his wife and had never been.

He didn't like that. He began pacing back and forth as he expressed a litany of things he felt were wrong with me. I remained quiet for the first few minutes. Finally, I had to interrupt him. If I was so terrible, why was he here? Why not let me go? He didn't even LIKE me!

He said what I already knew. He felt like I was his and that seemed to be where his reasoning stopped. I tried to stay calm. My calmness seemed to further irritate him. He began to get louder. I felt like he wanted to elicit a response.

A few of the gems he dropped at my mother's front door that evening included:

- I was a broken woman because at thirty I'd never had a child. (I'd had a birthday since trying to break it off after the wedding.)
- I was broke because I had to work and lived with my mother.

- I couldn't keep a man because once again I was going to be single.

He didn't like it when I pointed out that condoms were fairly inexpensive and birth control wasn't that hard to come by with insurance, which I had because of my job. Sure I was going to be single again but so was he. Did that make him a failure too? Was he a worse failure for having a baby mama who couldn't stand him and now a failed attempt at getting married?

I guess that's all I had to say. He asked for his ring back. I rushed inside to get the ring.

When I handed it to him I couldn't stop myself from taking a jab. I reminded him that he'd complained about buying my ring. A ring I chose for the blue stone and the clearance price. It was three hundred dollars with insurance coverage. I asked him which one of us was actually broke.

I also gave him back his credit card. The same card he'd made such a big about that thirteen dollar purchase over. I made sure to cut it up first. That added fuel to his angry fire. He began pacing in the street and yelling the rest of my perceived inadequacies. I felt momentary embarrassment. What must the neighbors be thinking? Strange thing to be concerned about at that moment but it definitely crossed my mind. According to him, I was terrible in bed as well. This was news to me. I asked him why he would borrow money to fly nearly nine hundred miles to see a woman you didn't like and didn't feel was physically satisfying. He had no answer for that.

Watching him yell and lose control was like pulling the last linchpin of his hold on me. When I went back into the house, my mother was crying. She wanted me to give him another chance. I couldn't believe her.

He began texting me but blocked my number so I couldn't respond to his attacks where he continued to insult me. I'm not proud of it but I had things to say so I emailed him. Mostly thanking him for showing his true colors and proving my choice to be a good one. His email responses alternated between asking me to stop and deriding me. The emails mentioned,

- He hoped that my next relationship resulted in my contracting HIV.

- He hoped I never had any children.

- According to him my brothers and I must have had an incestuous relationship for them to be willing to fight him. I finally stopped responding and decided that it was finally over. I would not engage in any way.

Lesson learned: Even if no one else understands your comfort and safety are reasons enough to choose to walk away.

CHAPTER 13

THE END OF IT

I wish I could say that I never heard from him again but that wasn't the case. Every so often he'd reach out to me. I would always cut off communication in whatever way he reached out. No social media, no emails, no calls, and no text. I needed a clean break for my sanity.

The aftermath of this taught me so much. I realized that I could start over whenever I wanted to. It also taught me who I could count on. I had family members who chose to believe that he couldn't possibly be that bad. According to them, he seemed too nice to be anything but great to me. That argument always made me think of the news footage after serial killers were caught. The neighbors always say how nice they were. How they would have never guessed. Even the spouses and children sometimes say that. It rankled me that they would trust a few casual encounters with someone who was essentially a stranger over me.

My mother did eventually come around and ask me if he'd ever hit me. When I told her he hadn't she seemed confused. She maintained that she would never want me to be with an abuser but she couldn't quite wrap her head around verbal and emotional abuse. She understood the concepts but she felt he was 'too nice' to be that kind of guy. I never could get her to let go of that thinking fully. She reasoned that she trusted my judgment to bring a good man to the family. Yet she didn't fully trust my judgment when I told her that wasn't the case.

When I left my mother's house I didn't tell her where my apartment was for fear that she'd tell him. My siblings were the only ones who knew. It took me over a year before I even considered dating again. I didn't trust myself to choose well. Intellectually I understood that it wasn't my fault but emotionally I didn't quite believe that. I had made a huge mistake the last time. I was unwilling to do that again.

It took me most of that year to work on myself and gain back my trust in me. I had to weed out the negative self-talk and build myself back up. This was a process. It wasn't easy or pretty but I got through it. I now understand what I want and I know I deserve it.

It took a year before I could admit that I wasn't married. I felt like I was a failure somehow. It took two years before I could speak publicly about the situation. When I did, I chose to post a video on Facebook. I explained that while there had been a ceremony there most certainly had been no marriage. I explained that I had made this decision because it was what I believed was best for me. Most of the feedback was supportive. One of his sisters commented. She felt that I was demonizing her brother. That wasn't my intent then and it isn't now.

One person sent me a message saying that he would like me to continue sharing my story. He had a friend who was killed by her husband in front of their two small children. He said that she'd tried to leave twice and her family and friends talked her into staying. He felt that maybe more people would listen to me since I'd lived through it.

One of my fears was that I wouldn't survive to tell this story. I was afraid that my story would become a made for TV movie where I could not speak for myself. Some have accused me of being dramatic. I don't listen to those people. There is a reason why TV shows like Fatal Attraction, Fatal Vows and Snapped will never run out of source material. I often find myself watching these shows and sighing in relief that I am not the subject on the screen.

Man may make someone a wonderful partner someday. I wasn't that person for him. There are things that I didn't speak of in this book out of respect for his family and mine. There are things that I did include though because if you're reading this you may see yourself in my experience. Your forever is not a toxic or hurtful relationship.

The point of this story is survival. A new last name is not worth your life. A shiny ring isn't a reason to die.

For me, it has been five years of being hypervigilant and holding myself accountable. As I am going over the final edits for this book, I am looking at my new baby girl. She was born happy and healthy. Her father is amazing and wonderful to us both. After all that I've been through I wouldn't say that I believe in happily ever after per se but I am happy. There is hope after heartache. You can walk away and choose yourself.

I promise that it isn't too late. I am a living breathing testament of that.

If you find that you feel unsafe in your relationship. PLEASE LEAVE. If someone you claim to love tells you they are fearful in their relationship, please believe them!

Lesson learned: It's human to make mistakes. Forgive yourself for choosing them over you. It's the only way to grow past it.

LESSONS LEARNED

If it seems too good to be true it is ok to be skeptical.

Speak up. Don't shrink yourself for anyone. When you start to see the inconsistencies don't pretend they aren't there. It helps no one. Don't let anyone talk you into staying in bad relationships, not even yourself.

Sometimes outsiders see the truth, even when you don't want to acknowledge it. It's ok to listen to that feedback.

You can't force a relationship no matter how hard you try. Choose relationships and spaces where you can blossom.

It's never too late to have an exit strategy. You can change your mind at any time.

You deserve someone who puts you first in their decision making. It isn't too much to expect to be a priority in your partner's life.

Your experience is your own and it is valid. Your loved ones may think they are doing what's right for you. You know better than anyone what is right for you. Trust your instinct.

Even if no one else understands, your comfort and safety are reasons enough to choose to walk away.

It's human to make mistakes. Forgive yourself for choosing them over you. It's the only way to grow past it.

SOURCES AND HELPFUL LINKS

https://en.wikipedia.org/wiki/Cycle_of_abuse

https://www.domesticviolenceroundtable.org/domestic-violence-cycle.html

https://www.womenscenteryfs.org/index.php/get-info/prevention/education/14-cycle-of-violence

Get help at thehotline.org or call

1-800-799-7233

1-800-787-3224 (TTY)

www.ingramcontent.com/pod-product-compliance
Lightning Source LLC
Chambersburg PA
CBHW021205090426
42740CB00008B/1237